TO THE ONES I LOVE

You are my INSPIRATION, GUIDES, TEACHERS, LAUGHTER, and most of all MY LOVE.

TIPPIE – From the MOMENT, I held you in my arms, I knew a STAR was born.

DAISY – You are WATER that brings LIFE to a tree in the DESERT.

SPIRIT – You are my TEACHER, my INSPIRATION for hope. With YOU, anything is POSSIBLE.

NALA – My SWEETEST little girl. You are the LIGHT that SHINES in the darkest of NIGHTS.

JACKSON – My MENTOR, CLOSEST FRIEND, and CONFIDENT.

I CHERISH every waking MOMENT with you ALL.
MOM

Author

Nyx Nightshade is a mom, entrepreneur, energy healer, and published author. Her animals and actual live events inspire her books. She is certified in Reiki, Blue Stone & Crystal Healing. She lives in Toronto, Ontario, with her horses and donkeys.

Illustrator

Andre Vitali is an internationally acclaimed illustrator / graphic designer who has lived and worked in Italy and Ireland. Andre began developing his drawing skills as a child. He Graduated in 2005 from L' Accademia Delle Belle Arti University. He lives in Monreale, Italy.

Narrator

Angela Clark is a voice artist. She has enjoyed voicing many different genres and thoroughly enjoys every aspect of voice-over. However, audiobook narration was her starting point. She always enjoyed reading, so audiobook narration was a natural progression of that passion.
She's had the privilege of working directly with several different publishers and many authors.
Angela has narrated over 150 audiobooks and over 200 hours of audio dramas.

STAY CONNECTED!

Tippie-Doo's website at www.tippie-doo.com

📷 @tippiedoo   ▶ @TippieDoo   📌 @TippieDoo

f @tippie.doo   ♪ @tippiedoo   🐦 @tippie_doo

Scan the QR code to access the digital version of the book.

It is fully narrated in the children's voices by Angela Clark
and illustrated by Andre Vitali.

Copyright @ 2023 by Tippie-Doo Media Corp Canada. All rights reserved.
All related titles and logos are the trademark of Tippie-Doo.
Printed in the United States of America
This book may be used for educational and entertainment purposes only.
No part in this book may be used or reproduced in whatsoever anyway or manner without written permission.

For information address, you may visit www.tippie-doo.com

www.tippie-doo.com

TIPPIE & NALA'S

CLEANING DAY

BY NYX NIGHTSHADE

ILLUSTRATED BY ANDREA VITALI
NARRATED BY ANGELA CLARK

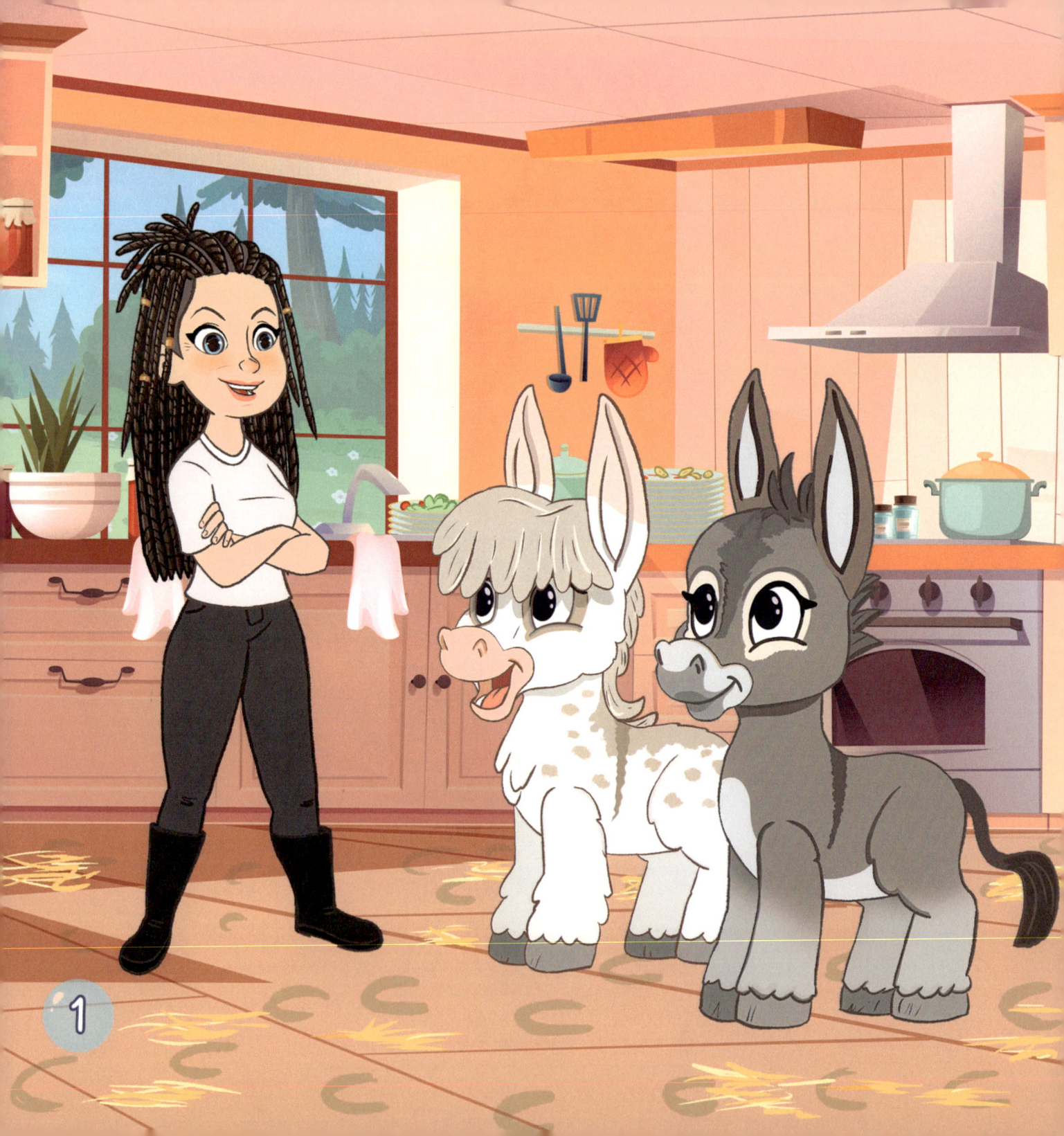

Mama woke up early and wandered off to the kitchen. She opened the cupboards and saw they were bare. "Oh goodness, I need to go shopping. Kids, I must take a ride to the grocery store," she called out.

"Why Mama?" asked Nala.

"I need to buy hay cubes, carrots, apples, and some things for myself. We're almost out," said Mama. "My princess, Nala, take care of your brother and make sure he stays out of mischief!"

"Okay, Mama, I will," replied Nala.

Mama grabbed her purse, and out the door she went.

"Hey, Tippie, let's clean the house for Mama before she gets home," said Nala. "This will make her so happy, and I'm sure we will get extra carrots for our dinner!"

"Nala!" Tippie looked at her with a quizzical brow. "I thought you wanted to do something nice?"

"Well of course I do, Tippie," she replied. "Mama takes such good care of us, but..."

"Oh, you little donkey devil, I like how you think!" Tippie snickered-his hands covering his mouth. "Nala, do you remember the last time we tried to do that? What a disaster that was!"

"It's okay. This time we will be more careful. I'll clean the dishes and mop the floors, and you can do the laundry and clean the bedroom. We will finish in no time," said Nala. "You know how to use the machine, right, Tippie?"

"Well, of course, I do!" Tippie replied confidently. "I've watched Mama a hundred times!"

So, Nala galloped off to the kitchen while Tippie trotted to the laundry room.

"Hmmm... let's see. I put the soap in first, then the clothes, and press the wash button. Yes, that's it!" Tippie said happily. "I knew I paid attention!"

The water started to rise, so he set off to his next chore.

"While the clothes are in the washer, I will start the bedroom," Tippie mumbled. "I'll fluff her pillows and tighten the sheets- this should be easy!"

Tippie took the corner of the pillow with his teeth and started waving it up and down in the air. But couldn't get it fluffy enough.

He quickly turned around and began to buck the pillow, and suddenly, POOF! The pillow exploded—feathers flying in the air!

"Oh, donkey-doodles, I kicked too hard and made a bigger mess!"

Suddenly, a BIG BANG came from the laundry room. **BOOM! BOOM! BOOM!** "Oh goodness, what now?" he shrieked. "Tippie, what on earth is going on back here?" Nala neighed out loud. "I can feel the floor shaking!"
"Nala, I'm in so much trouble!" he cried loudly. "Look at all the mess I made!"

"Tippie, the laundry machine is bubbling over, and there's water all over the floor!" she shouted. "Did you not close the lid?"

"Yes, I did! Ahh, well, maybe...no," replied Tippie.

"I asked you if you knew how to use the machine!" Nala said furiously.

"Well, I do. I watched Mama many times!" he replied.

"TIPPIE!!!!" she neighed. "You should have just asked me, it would have saved you all this trouble!"

"I'm sorry, I just wanted to do my best," Tippie sadly said, looking down.

Nala looked over at Tippie and saw teardrops falling from his eyes, making her feel very sad.

"I'm sorry, I didn't mean to become angry with you, but you should have been honest with me, and we could have worked together. That's what teamwork is all about," Nala gently said. "Let's clean this up first, and then we can tidy up the bedroom afterwards."

"Well...., about that...," said Tippie.

Nala saw the look on Tippie's face, so she quickly trotted to the bedroom. Tippie right behind her and saw feathers all over the floor. She put her hoofs on her cheeks and said, "Oh, my goodness, what did you do here?"

"I wanted to fluff Mama's pillows by waving them in the air. But I couldn't get them fluffy enough, so, I tried to buck them, and well... the pillow broke open! Now I have feathers all over the floor!" replied Tippie.

Nala burst into laughter. "It's okay! The same thing happened to me once before, then Mama and I ended up in a pillow fight. It was lots of fun!"

"Oh, that's easy!" Tippie waved his hoof-like he had it all figured out.

He started to roll all over the floor and was covered in bubbles from head to toe! Nala laughed so hard that she fell to the floor with her legs straight in the air.

"Tippie, it's no wonder Mama can't stay angry with you too long. It's because you make her laugh!"

"She won't be laughing if we don't hurry up and clean this mess! So please help me, Nala!" he pleaded.

Just then, they heard the car pulling into the driveway.
"Oh, my goodness, oh my goodness, what do we do?" shrieked Tippie. "We still have the bedroom to finish!"

Mama opened the door with a handful of bags. Tippie and Nala yelled, "SURPRISE!"

"Oh, Tippie, what happened? You are covered in bubbles!" Mama chuckled.

"Nala bathed me, and look, Mama- I'm all clean!"

Mama looked at Tippie curiously and then at Nala. "What a beautiful job cleaning the kitchen. The floor is sparkling!"

"Thank you, Mama! I polished it myself!" Tippie leaped in the air with excitement.

"Yes, I can see that!" said Mama, grinning from ear to ear.

Mama headed for the bedroom, and suddenly Nala and Tippie jumped in front of her and yelled, "WAIT! We still need to finish this room. There was a little... well, we tried to..."

"HOLD IT!"

"I know exactly what you two did, and I must say... WE ARE DUE FOR A PILLOW FIGHT! Kids, let's play!" Mama screamed with excitement.

"OH BOY, Nala, you were right! This is awesome fun! Now, tell me, whose mama would allow you to clean and mess the house at the same time?"

Shortly after, Mama looked at them and said, "Kids, I want you to know how proud I am of you! I know how hard you both worked to make me happy. And yes, Tippie, I'm sure you had lots of fun rolling on the floor and cleaning up the bubbles from not closing the washing machine lid!"

Tippie looked down, blushing, and said, "Mama, I thought I could remember just by watching you."

"I'm proud you are eager to learn, but I must show you how. This way, things like this don't happen. But I will say, Tippie, you sure do shine!" Mama laughed. " Why don't we put the groceries away first, and then tidy the bedroom?"

"Mama, does this mean we can have a carrot before, during, and after dinner?" they both asked.

"Yes, of course," Mama giggled.

"Oh boy, you're the best!" they said, jumping up and down.

"Kids, I'm thankful for all the work you put in. Your teamwork is very much appreciated, and I had so much fun playing with you. I hope we do this again soon!"

www.ingramcontent.com/pod-product-compliance
Lightning Source LLC
Chambersburg PA
CBRC090902080526
44587CB00008B/176